Anger Man...
Stay Cool in ......

by Carol Hargreaves BEd,
Master Practicioner NLP

First Published
January 2007 in Great Britain by

Educational Printing Services Limited
Albion Mill, Water Street, Great Harwood, Blackburn BB6 7QR
Telephone: (01254) 882080   Fax: (01254) 882010
Email: enquiries@eprint.co.uk   Website: www.eprint.co.uk

© Carol Hargreaves

The moral right of the author has been asserted in accordance with the Copyright,
Designs and Patents Act 1988.

ISBN - 1-905637-06-3
ISBN - 13 978-1-905637-06-5

Anger Management
Stay Cool in School

If you have ever had a problem with getting wound up, losing your temper, or having violent and angry outbursts, then this book is for you. It will help you to understand why you had this problem and what you can do about changing it. In this book you will find out how to respond in different ways to the things that used to wind you up, to recognise and manage your emotions more effectively and to feel more confident about yourself from now on.

If you are a parent or have a mentoring role, which will enable you to encourage and motivate a young person in developing Emotional Literacy/Anger Management Skills, then there is support and advice for you here too. This book will provide you with a way of working that will help you to empower young people to develop new ways of responding in challenging situations and to handle their emotions more effectively. They will be able to maintain any changes they achieve over time even after you have finished working with them.

Contents

Chapter 1	What is Anger Management?	1
Chapter 2	How to Get the Most out of this Book	5
Chapter 3	Why Bother?	7
Chapter 4	Do Something Different	9
Chapter 5	Understanding Anger	17
Chapter 6	Your Own Anger Chart	23
Chapter 7	Make a Master Plan!	27
Chapter 8	Pick-and-Mix!	39
	Information, Telephone Numbers and Websites	62

1 What is Anger Management?

It's ok to get angry. We all do it. Anger is a normal human emotion that we all experience sometimes.

Our emotions are part of what makes us who we are. We love, we hate, we feel upset, feel relieved, get excited, feel down, feel worried, feel on top of the world, get angry as well as a multitude of other emotions throughout our lives. We might even feel all of those emotions within one day or within one hour... Even within a few minutes we can swing through a whole range of emotions. For example do you ever remember a time when you or a friend were accused of something you hadn't done? You may have experienced worry, confusion, amazement, disbelief, resentment, upset, anger... all within a couple of minutes.

So, anger is OK and normal and if you notice you are angry, it can be useful to you - a signal that something is wrong and you need to do something different - a great opportunity to make things better for you.

If your anger has become a problem, however, it is likely that you are experiencing the normal human emotion but more intensely or more frequently than is usual. It probably means that you have lost control, hurt yourself or others, had angry outbursts that have resulted in property being damaged, and said things that you normally know you should not say. You may have had problems at home, at school with other young people or teachers, outside school or at work. Perhaps it may even have been all of them? This may have caused you problems with being isolated or excluded from school, maintaining friendships, feeling disapproved of, being feared, getting grounded or banned from activities you like doing for example.

That's when it's not OK any more.

Mostly, the young people I meet who describe themselves as having an anger management problem tell me *"It's just how I am. I can't help it"*. I have heard that so many times... and it just is not true. The person who says it thinks it's true but it isn't. There are so many easy ways of breaking out of that pattern, giving yourself choices, so many ways of learning how to turn that anger down again so that you can regulate your behaviour and choose to do something different.

Anger Management is all about re-gaining control of your emotions, turning your responses back down to normal levels and getting on with doing the things you really want to do.

Everybody who follows the "**Stay Cool in School**" programme will be able to change how they used to react in situations that once got them angry. Other young people, like you, who have followed this programme say things like,

"It's a million times better."

and

"I just don't do that [kick off] any more."

Their teachers say things like,

"You wouldn't recognise him - it's like he's a different boy."

Their parents may say,

"I can't believe it - it's like I've got my daughter back."

What do you think people will say to you?

Chapter 1

You too will be able to see a difference for yourself, very soon after you have begun. You too will be able to stay cool at times when you used to feel angry. We are going to concentrate on staying cool in school, but of course the ideas in this book work wherever you are and whoever you are with.

I will help you to find ways of managing your anger, by noticing what caused it and dealing with both the cause and the physical effects of being angry. Because this way of managing your anger really works and is about helping yourself, instead of just going through the motions because someone says you have got to, you will soon find that you can **Stay Cool in School**. You will feel good about yourself, protect yourself from the hurt someone intended you to feel and avoid the consequences of getting so angry. That would be great wouldn't it? You get what you want. You stay safe. You stay in control. You get noticed for all the right reasons.

That's Anger Management.

2 How to Get the Most out of this Book

Before you go any further, you will need to decide how to use this book so that you get the most out of it.

There are a couple of decisions to make.

> Are you going to go from cover to cover or just dip in?

You could read the book from cover to cover - and that could be a really thorough and well structured way of going about it. I say this because the book is written especially for you and the ideas are presented in a way that build up on each other, step by step, until by the end you have everything you need in what I consider to be the best order possible.

However, you could choose to just dip into it and find something new that is immediately useful to you. Therefore, if you want quick results, you could go straight to Chapter 8 Pick-and-Mix! and find a strategy that seems to hit the mark for you or appeals to you in some way. If you choose this way of using the book, then you will give yourself a quick boost, a head start on things. Then you could go back to the beginning and do more reading afterwards.

Are you going to read alone or get help?

It may help you to really get the most out of the book if you read it with someone else or at least discuss it with someone you trust. We can all achieve more with help or support than alone. If you can find someone to help you, they can sometimes see things from a different perspective to you, see the "the bigger picture", help you make sense of something complicated or just be someone who will listen and discuss your ideas. Sometimes it just helps if someone encourages you not to give up, to carry on trying. If you haven't already got someone to help you, it would be useful to first think who you might like to help you and then ask. If you don't ask, they will never know that you need this help. So ask. If they can't do it, for whatever reason, ask someone else.

Alternatively, you might choose to read this book on your own. This means that you don't have to discuss your difficulties with anyone and you will be able to work out for yourself privately what to do about them. It might also be that you can't find anyone to help or don't trust anyone enough. In that case, it's better to read the book alone than not at all.

3 Why Bother?

You are probably reading this book because you have had difficulty controlling your anger in school.

If this is the case, then you will have experienced some sanctions or punishments, some regrets and some embarrassment. You may have been isolated, excluded or have been in constant trouble because of angry outbursts - when the things you have said and/or done went out of control. You may have been banned from a school trip or not allowed to do a work experience because it was thought that you couldn't keep your temper cool enough. You may have had difficulty with friends - perhaps people you liked have avoided you. Perhaps your parents or carers have refused to let you do the things you liked as a punishment.

You may have blamed others for your actions -

"Just get rid of that boy - he winds me up - if it wasn't for him I'd be all right."

or

"If I didn't have to go to maths - I hate it - things would be fine."

or

"It's just that teacher. She's got it in for me."

Sound familiar? It's OK - I hear that stuff a lot - but do you know something?......if I got rid of that boy, or arranged for you to get out of that class or changed your teacher to another one, that wouldn't be the end of it. The next time someone else pushed those same buttons, or the next time you were finding something difficult to understand in class, or the next time a teacher seemed to be picking you out, the same would happen again. It's not about them.

It's about you.

You might think a quick fix would be OK.

Why not paper over the cracks and make surface level changes? And it might work for a while, but it's not just about this lesson, this week, this month or even this term.

It's about the rest of your life.

It's about learning how to manage your emotions, your anger, more effectively - not just for now, but throughout your whole life. It's about learning how to cope with set-backs, people not liking you, finding something difficult to do, being disappointed or failing at something. It's an essential life skill that maybe you didn't have before but after reading this book, you soon will have.

It's about doing something different to whatever you were doing before.

You might think,

"It can't be that easy".

But it is. Read on and find out.

4 Do Something Different

This book will help you get back on track, to help you control your anger so that you can **Stay Cool in School**.

I will take you through the book, helping you to understand about anger in general and more specifically your own anger.

Only when you understand why you were doing what you were doing, and how you were doing it, will you be able to work out how to overcome it.

I will help you work out exactly what it is that you can change so that you can break down any stuck patterns in your behaviour - and do something different and better from now on.

Just think about this:

If what you are doing isn't working
Do something different
Do anything different
And you will get a different result.

This helps me to explain a really important basic idea - and I am sharing it with you now because it is helpful for you to understand it too - that is, just do something different - any little thing will do for a start - and things will be different. The thing you do differently doesn't have to be a big thing, but it will release you from your own stuck pattern and you will get a different result.

And that's a good thing to understand because sometimes when we have a major task to complete, it can seem overwhelming, making it difficult to start. We all know that's true and I can think of many examples like room-tidying, completing coursework, applying for a job, when the task seems so overwhelming that you don't know how or where to start. So breaking it all down into smaller chunks and making a little start - doing a little thing different - is a great way of overcoming that barrier to starting. Then the next step is easier and so on!

So follow the process I have devised for you in this book - it breaks the task down into bite-size chunks, takes little steps, one at a time and it allows you to make your own choices - ones that you feel you can realistically do, and ones that will create meaningful change for you in your own world.

Then you will be able to move on from the problems you have had, leave behind the punishments and regrets and step forward successfully to get on with the life you really want for yourself. Imagine that!

Here's another way of thinking about the same idea ....

There's an ad on the television for a car with a new diesel engine. I mention it, because I love the words [and it has one of those tunes that you just cannot get out of your head!]. The words go like this - if you can imagine them sung in a really cheesy American accent:

Hate somethin'
Change somethin'
Hate somethin'
Change somethin'
Make somethin' better

You may recognise the ad or the words but if you don't it doesn't matter! You can say these words rhythmically to yourself in your head if you like. I love the words because they help to explain the process that you have to follow in order to 'unstick' a problem and make something better... you need to recognise that something you have been doing is causing you a problem, change something, and so make things better.

Read through the next section and fill in (photocopy if necessary) the chart on page 15 with your own information. Don't just do this in your head; you must write on your copy of the chart. When completed, this will help you to see how things have been, how you would prefer them to be and will lay down the basis of a map of how to get from one to the other successfully.

Hate Something

Start with the "HATE SOMETHING" column and fill it all in as much as you can about the problem you have had. Take yourself back to the most recent or most serious incident. Remember now the things you said, and how exactly you said them, the things you did and exactly how you did them, what happened as a result and the consequences you have had to accept. On a scale of 1-10, where 10 is as bad as it can get, rate how serious this incident was. Who noticed things were really bad for you? How do you know they noticed?

Change Something

For the moment, you will need to leave the question-mark in this section. Leave it blank - but soon you will be able to complete the bullet points by making a 3-Step Master Plan. You will choose 3 things that you can realistically do differently from the strategies in Chapter 8 Pick-and-Mix! - I will guide you and help you to decide what to do and very importantly when and how to do it. With my help, you will form a plan that will work for you and you will very quickly be able to see, hear and feel the difference. When you carry out your plan, you will begin to notice the differences in yourself and how people are responding towards you. They need only be little things but even so they will 'unstick' the old stuck patterns you had and things will be different.

Make Something Better

Now move on to the "MAKE SOMETHING BETTER" column. Picture vividly in your mind how you would prefer things to be. Make it into a mini-movie, a success film. Make it bright and in colour, run the film as if on a huge screen in front of you with a soundtrack of voices and maybe even music. Notice what you see, hear and feel, as vividly as you can. Who do you think will notice the changes you have made? How will you know they are pleased for you? Now identify a timescale... when do you want this to have happened by?

HATE SOMETHING ➔ CHANGE SOMETHING ➔ MAKE SOMETHING BETTER

About the problem you have had

What you said _____

What you did _____

What were the consequences _____

On a scale of 1 – 10 where 10 is as bad as it gets, rate how serious this incident was

1 2 3 4 5 6 7 8 9 10

Who has noticed how difficult things have been? _____

How would you prefer things to be

How will you know when things are better?
What will you:
See? _____
Hear? _____
Feel? _____

Make a success movie in your head – like watching a film of yourself when things are better. Make sure it is just right. Go over it again until it is.

On a scale of 1 – 10 as before, rate how you expect to feel when things are better like this.

1 2 3 4 5 6 7 8 9 10

Who will notice your success? _____

When do you want this by? _____

So now you have completed the chart, you have a clear idea of what the problem has been and a clear picture of how you would prefer things to be. All that remains to be done is to work out how to make the journey from one to the other.

Do Something Different 15

5 Understanding Anger

In this chapter I am going to help you to understand the psychological and biological processes of anger. These processes are the same for everybody and I am sure that as you read on, you will recognise that you are basically just like anyone else who has got angry. We need to do this because when you understand these processes more clearly, you will be able to choose the best new strategies to help you to keep them under control more effectively.

Let's start by getting a clear picture of the psychological and biological processes of anger. This diagram shows what usually happens when people get angry - and it's roughly the same for everyone.

Follow the diagram as you read and as you do so, think about how it applies to you. Be open about this - you need to be truthful with yourself to achieve the transformation you want.

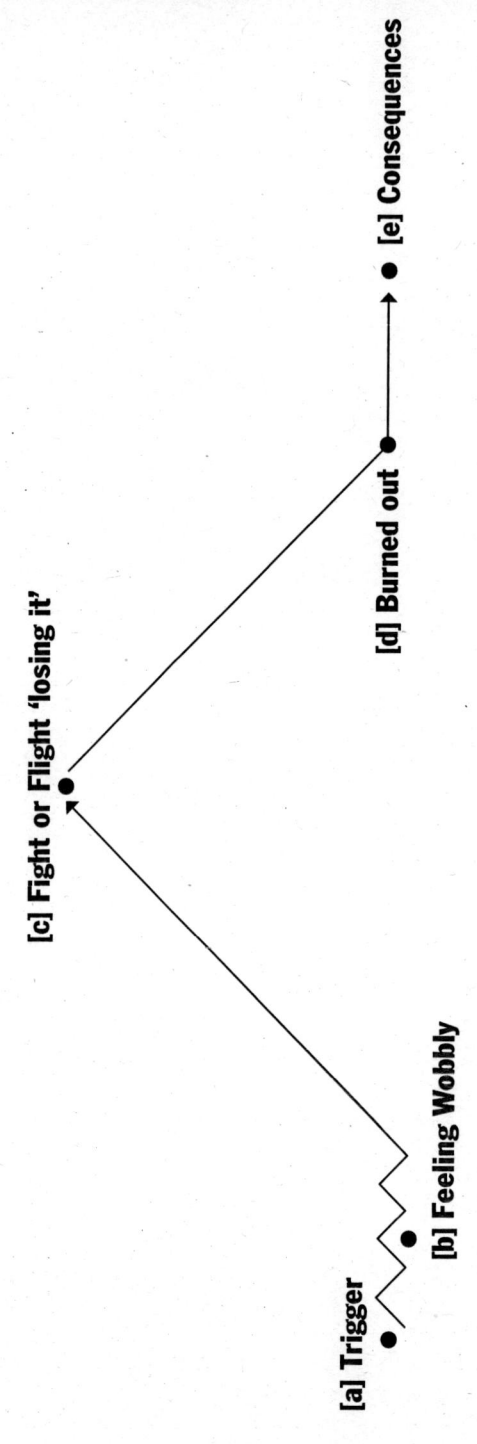

[a] Trigger

At the very beginning of this process, something acts as a trigger to start off an emotional response in you. Usually it is something you could interpret as a threat, put-down or challenge in some way - a look, a certain word, a tone of voice, insults, pushing, cheating, work that's too hard or too easy are all examples. It is likely to be just a small thing - but that small thing really winds you up. Sometimes when it is connected with something that has happened before, your response to the trigger is even stronger.

[b] Feeling "Wobbly"

When that trigger has started off an emotional response in you, you may start to feel what I describe as "wobbly"- that is, a bit agitated or wound up. You might notice differences in your body like your heart beating faster, butterflies in your stomach, palms sweating, but you can still cope with the situation. You are able to stay in control at this point, and you can still reason with yourself. You have choices. You can still say to yourself good advice like,

"Oh-oh...cool it!"

and you can still listen to that advice. You can choose to ignore someone and you can just avoid any further exposure to the trigger by walking away.

[c] Fight or Flight "losing it"

If there is another trigger, or if you have been doing some unhelpful self-talk that has wound you up further, then the Fight or Flight response starts. This response is triggered by a perceived threat and it is meant to be helpful to you. Adrenaline rushes round your body and causes sugars and fats to be made available to your muscles for a burst of extra energy. It also causes the heart to beat more strongly and blood to be diverted from your digestive system to your muscles. This response is meant to help you to "fight" the danger or to take "flight" and run away to safety. It's a survival mechanism that worked well in cave man days. Imagine a scenario where a woolly mammoth is charging towards a cave man. This danger triggered the Fight or Flight response and the cave man had a burst of energy to help him run away faster than he usually could or to throw his spear more strongly than usual so that he killed the charging mammoth and had it for his tea. However, we rarely face such real dangers in modern times and the Fight or Flight response is often mistakenly triggered in stressful situations. There are two main problems with this. One is that with adrenaline pumping round your body, we get really "pumped up" and all that extra energy must be used up. Secondly, the adrenaline doesn't only have physical effects, it also shuts down the rational or thinking part of your brain and you go temporarily beyond your own control. For the cave man, great! This helped him face incredible danger, shutting down his fear to ensure he could do what he needed to do in order to survive. However, not so great for you as you become unreasoning, irrational and driven in survival mode to lash out at whatever you perceived was the threat. You may say and do things that normally you know you shouldn't or wouldn't do...fighting, lashing out, throwing things, storming out, pushing furniture over, breaking things, shouting insults, swearing. It could possibly be all of those things at once!

[d] Burned out

When you have burned up all the extra energy that the adrenaline rush gave you, you start to calm down and re-gain control. It is estimated that it takes about 20 minutes to be fully back in control and in a calm state. Most people now feel very uncomfortable at having been out of control at this stage and will probably feel low in energy, washed out and tired. Perhaps you have embarrassed yourself or someone else, hurt someone or damaged property. You may be filled with regrets and wish that you hadn't done or said the things you did. However, what's done is done and what's said cannot be unsaid!

There is a small minority of young people who don't experience this "down" time after an outburst. They enjoy the adrenaline rush, the "buzz" and are willing to risk the consequences - even seeking out further opportunities to get the "buzz" again, until these consequences become very bad indeed and something they enjoy or value very much, like their freedom, is taken away.

[e] Consequences

So, finally, there are the consequences. How serious these are will depend on whose rules you have broken, who got hurt, what got damaged. You may be
punished with isolation, exclusion, being grounded, or disapproval from teachers, other young people and parents. Sometimes other young people may be scared to be friendly with you or avoid you in case you flare up again. You may be the subject of some humiliating wind-ups from other young people trying to score a few points or have some entertainment at your expense. If you have broken the law or violated a court order, there may be more serious consequences - punishments that take away your freedoms and choices.

6 Your Own Anger Chart

Now we will relate all of that to you and the problems you have had with anger. You will develop a detailed description of your own angry responses using this as a guide.

Concentrating on one specific, recent incident, you are going to create a film in your head of how it really happened. You will need to look at the same incident over and over again, like having it on a DVD that you can turn on, turn off, slow down, speed up, rewind, or fast forward as many times as you like. You will be able to pause and really look in detail at specific parts of the film and sometimes even imagine stepping into the film to get a better recollection of what it was really like to be there at that time. This will help you fill in your own Anger Chart accurately.

Important: Before you start answering the questions on pages 24-25 practise using the DVD and especially the off switch. Practise by using another more pleasant film in your head of a special place you have been to. The off switch should blank out the film completely or make the picture small, black and white, still and far away from you. When you can do that easily, watch your film of a specific recent incident in detail and answer the questions below. Use the off switch if you start to experience too much of your anger as you watch the film. Shut it all down instantly by using the off button on the DVD, get up, walk around and give your full attention to something else. Then try again, but this time watch the film as if its on a screen that is further away, across the room.

Now you are ready to complete your own Anger Chart. Photocopy the chart if necessary and answer the following questions as fully as you can, writing in the boxes or on a separate piece of paper if there isn't enough room. Writing this down will help you to get things in the right order, focus your attention and move from a good general idea about anger to understanding your own anger more clearly. Be as exact as you can, going back through your film of a recent incident as often as you need to, pausing and re-winding whenever necessary to get the information you need.

Anger Chart

[a] Triggers
Start watching the DVD from the very beginning. Go back to before everything kicked off. It may have been something very simple or small, like a look or a tone of voice or 'the way he nudged my desk'. Look again, and notice exactly what it was in detail.

[b] Feeling Wobbly
Watch the film and notice that at this stage you are still in control. What are the first signs that things are starting to bother you? Notice your facial expression, your movements, gestures. Where in your body do you first notice something is different? What do you say to yourself in your head? What do you do? Where do you go? How do you feel?

Anger Chart (cont.)

[c] Fight or Flight - "losing it"

Notice what you do, how you move, your facial expression now. Listen to the things you say and how you say them. Notice the things you say to yourself in your head. Important: use the off switch at any time. Now step into the film for just a few moments as if you are really there now and notice how it feels when you are "losing it". Step back out now.

[d] Burned Out

Now go to after the incident has finished. Notice how you look, what you are doing, how you move. Listen out for the things you are saying - to others and to yourself - notice how it feels.

[e] Consequences

Move forward to where you become aware of the consequences of what you did. Step back in to the film now as if you are really there and experience fully how you feel. List the consequences - for you at home, at school, with friends and other young people. How has this incident affected your life? Step back out now. Make sure you have stepped out of the film properly. To be sure, give your attention to three different things you can see around you. Notice them in detail. Good.

7 Make a Master Plan!

In this chapter we will pull together everything we have done so far and develop your own 3-Step Master Plan to enable you to start out on a journey that will see you successfully travel from the old problems you had with anger and towards staying cool in school. You have read the book so far and you now know:

What was going wrong and how you were doing that.
[Hate Something]

You now also know what you want instead.
[Make Something Better]

This chapter is all about moving from one to the other....

It is time to start that journey now - with a Master Plan that will show you how!
[Change Something]

I will now hand you the keys to your success - the things that will make that journey happen.

Follow the steps I ask you to make and by the end of the chapter you will have a clear Master Plan of 3 new strategies that meet your needs exactly. These strategies will work for you and provide you with a path between Hate Something and Make Something Better. They are the "what to do and how" and will get you away from where you were and get you moving towards where you want to be. Use the chart on pages 31 – 33 to help you identify exactly what it is you used to do and then work out what to do instead.

Whenever you are making a plan to change something for the better, it is useful to bear these guidelines in mind. Think about them when you are putting your Master Plan together. It needs to:

- be about what **you** did - not what somebody else did
- have small **achievable** steps
- be **useful**
- make a **big** difference to you
- be **flexible** and subject to alterations if necessary
- **work**

The three step Master Plan will consist of identifying one aspect from each of these sections of your own Anger Chart.

Triggers
Feeling Wobbly
Fight or Flight "Losing it"

Think about each one in turn - start at the top with **Triggers** then work downwards, completing **Feeling Wobbly** and **Fight or Flight "losing it"**.

In each section:

Look at your description of what you used to do. It might help to look again at your film as you do so. Choose one aspect - remember it can be a small thing to start off with - and circle it with a coloured pen or pencil.

For example you might look at the **Triggers** section and notice you used to start to react when someone looked at you in a certain way.

Enter that onto your photocopy of the Master Plan on page 31 under HATE SOMETHING - What I did. Put in as much detail as you can remember.

Go to the **Pick-and-Mix!** chapter and find a strategy that you think might be useful for that particular situation and that will enable you to stop that happening in the same way again. Read through and talk about the alternatives, the choices you have. You could try several strategies out before you make up your mind. You must feel comfortable with your choice. When you have chosen, enter this in the second column CHANGE SOMETHING - what to do instead. Repeat that now, to complete the **Feeling Wobbly** and **Fight or Flight "losing it"** sections.

Now...

You have three new strategies. All these strategies work well.

But they only work when you use them.

So **Use them**. They will make a big difference to you.

You may only ever need to use the Triggers strategy to help you combat your response to a trigger.

Pay special attention to this strategy.

If you do this strategy successfully every time, you will never need to use the other two!

MASTER PLAN 1

HATE SOMETHING What I Did	CHANGE SOMETHING What to Do Instead	MAKE SOMETHING BETTER How Well Did It Work

Triggers

Make a Master Plan!

MASTER PLAN 2

	HATE SOMETHING What I Did	CHANGE SOMETHING What to Do Instead	MAKE SOMETHING BETTER How Well Did It Work
Feeling Wobbly			

MASTER PLAN 3

HATE SOMETHING What I Did	CHANGE SOMETHING What to Do Instead	MAKE SOMETHING BETTER How Well Did It Work
Losing it		

How Well Did it Work?

Every time you use a strategy, you need to enter something into the third column about how it went. You will know that the strategy went well for you if the end result was different, if it has disrupted the old patterns and resulted in something better in some way. Use these symbols to give an impression of how well you think the strategy worked...

Great! Do this more   Do it again but a bit differently   Try something else

If the strategy went well - **do it more!**

Keep all strategies that work and do them whenever they are useful. Reconsider those that could have been better now.

If it worked but it could have been better, you may want to **do it again but a bit differently**. Keep the strategy but just think - what might make it more successful next time? For instance, you could decide to start the strategy earlier or be more detailed about exactly how, where, when and with whom to do it so that you will be more successful.

If it didn't work at all, or in the way you expected, you may decide to **try something else**. Just check first in case there is something you could just do a bit differently to make it work better for you. If you still want to try something else **make a Plan B**.

To make a Plan B go back to the Pick and Mix and select a new strategy to use. Complete the chart on the next page, only filling in strategies that you want to change. Use the same symbols as before to help you get an impression of how well it went. Once again, make sure you **keep all strategies that went well**.

Reconsider any strategy that could have been better, try to work out just what you could do differently to make it more successful. Think very hard about this before you decide to try something else. If you need to, you can always make a **Plan C**!

PLAN B

Triggers	HATE SOMETHING What I Did	CHANGE SOMETHING What to Do Instead	MAKE SOMETHING BETTER How Well Did It Work

PLAN B

	HATE SOMETHING What I Did	CHANGE SOMETHING What to Do Instead	MAKE SOMETHING BETTER How Well Did It Work
Feeling Wobbly			

Make a Master Plan!

PLAN B

HATE SOMETHING What I Did	CHANGE SOMETHING What to Do Instead	MAKE SOMETHING BETTER How Well Did It Work

Losing it

8 Pick-and-Mix!

This chapter contains proven, reliable and effective strategies that when you use them in the right place and at the right time will help you on your journey to overcoming the problems you have had with managing your anger.

You must pick just three of them to put in your Master Plan. You need to choose one strategy for each of the sections, **Triggers**, **Feeling Wobbly** and **Fight or Flight "losing it"**. Enter them into your Master Plan (pages 31 – 33) and work out exactly what, when, where, how and with whom you are going to do them. The strategies you choose will provide you with alternative ways of thinking, feeling and behaving that when you use them will begin your journey from where you were to where you want to be.

When you use them, they will make a big difference quickly.

You could choose strategies that will help you to stay cool, even if someone is winding you up, or build up your ability to feel calm quickly at any time. You may choose to develop your ability to easily ignore taunts that used to bother you. You could choose to practise how to act as if you are more confident than you really are, in order to stop bullying. Whichever strategies you choose to do, you must be persistent and determined to make them work. Even though they are very simple, straightforward and common-sense when you know how to do them, most of the strategies will be new to you and **you will need to practise them.**

You will soon feel that you are making progress on your journey and when you are becoming more confident, more able to control your emotions effectively and can more often than not successfully stay cool in school, then you really are getting there!

Strategy 1 The oh-oh button

Useful for:

When you are in danger of doing what you always used to do. It's a warning signal, a pattern-breaker, a strategy that interrupts a stuck pattern so that you have a chance to do something different instead of getting swept along with what you used to do.

This strategy is exceptionally useful, easy to do and effective. It is well worth trying if you are unsure what else to do or can't decide. So - imagine you have an oh-oh button in the middle of your forehead. You will need this button to sound a warning for you to stop and take note. When you use it, it will warn you to notice that you are falling into an old stuck pattern that you no longer want.

For instance, if someone calls you a name and you start to get angry about it the way you used to, leading inevitably to **"losing it"** you need your oh-oh button to signal a warning to you to break the old pattern and do something different. At this stage, you are still in control and able to make good decisions about what you are doing.

Just picture this button now.

What colour is it? What shape? Is it smooth or rough, flat or ridged? Shiny or dull? How does it warn you? Perhaps it makes a warning siren sound? Or perhaps it turns on the voice of an advisor, a voice you will listen to, that says something helpful like "Do something different", "Stop now!" or "Time to go!"
Or perhaps it changes colour or flashes on and off?
It needs to work for you - so make it just right for you now.

As with all the strategies, it is very important to know the right time to start it so that it can be effective for you. How will you know when it is exactly the right time to be most useful to you? Think about that now so that you are prepared and ready to use it when you really need it. Think of a specific moment - it needs to be early enough in a situation so that you are still able to pay attention to its warning. Remember - once you have the adrenaline rushing round your body and you are losing it, it is too late. By then, you will not be able to pay attention to the warning and do something different. For example, it could be as soon as you spot a particular person coming towards you. Or when you first notice them using a tone of voice. Or the first nudge as someone knocks your desk as they walk past.

At this early stage, once you have paid attention to the warning of the oh-oh button, then you will be easily able to interrupt the old pattern and choose to do something different.

Strategy 2 Auditory, visual and kinaesthetic distraction

Useful for:

Stopping an old, unwanted response to a Trigger.

There are actually three distinct sets of strategies here. All you need to do is to work out whether your **Trigger** is a sound [an auditory trigger], a sight [a visual trigger] or a movement [a kinaesthetic trigger]. Once you have worked out what used to trigger off an angry reaction in you, what kicked it all off, you can start to work out how to respond in a different, more useful way.

Triggers fall into 3 distinct categories:

- Auditory Triggers - something you hear.
- Visual Triggers - something you see, for example a colour, flash of light, the look on someone's face, eye contact, gestures, clothing style.
- Kinaesthetic Triggers - a movement or action, for example a nudge, pulling your jumper, moving your work across the desk.

Often the trigger is a small, simple thing like a look or a word or a nudge. This simple beginning can often set a pattern of thoughts going which interprets the trigger in a very negative way, like

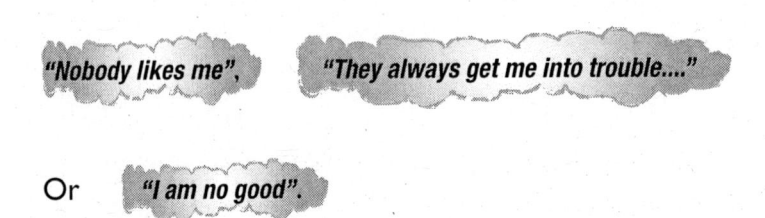

"Nobody likes me",   *"They always get me into trouble...."*

Or   *"I am no good"*.

This pattern of thoughts is unhelpful and accelerates or turns up your old response. It may be that the person doesn't realise what it is they are doing to upset you or why you respond in this way. On the other hand, when someone has discovered that they can wind you up in this way, they may do it just for the fun of it, making them feel powerful. Work out what your own trigger was and choose the strategy now that will stop that happening any more.

Auditory Triggers - something you hear:

For example - sounds, particular words, tones of voice.

One example of an extreme response to a particular word was a young man I worked with who could easily be wound up by other students using the word 'gay'. Once they discovered this, they said it to him every day and every day got the same extreme and out of control reaction. The young man was in a great deal of trouble for fighting and "losing it" at school. The teachers didn't know why he was doing this and were only dealing with the young man's violent and aggressive behaviour. Of course the students who were winding him up by calling him gay weren't in any trouble at all.

Sometimes when we interpret a **tone of voice** as being sneering, mocking or critical it can trigger off an angry reaction. An example of this might be if there is a particular lesson that you struggle with, either finding it boring or too difficult, in which you feel the teacher criticises you or picks on you. That tone of voice can trigger off an angry response that can result in disruption of lessons as you shout or answer back, or storm out angrily.

Whether the auditory trigger is a word, tone of voice, or any other sound, you will need to tone down your response to it. The word will still be used, the critical tone of voice still happen, but you can choose not to interact with them. That way, you stay just as calm as before and they feel momentarily confused or surprised and move onto something else.

Instead of interacting with an auditory trigger, you can distract yourself by giving your auditory attention to something else. This is not the same as saying "just ignore it". It's different and works better.

There are several easy ways to distract your auditory attention for you to try. You could switch on a tune in your head. A favourite song that you can easily turn on would be best. Sometimes it could be useful to choose a song that has words which are appropriate to the situation, like Daniel Beddingfield's "Gotta get through this", "Beautiful" by Christine Aguilera or one that is funny like "Amarillo". As you listen to the song, you will find it impossible to pay very much attention to any other sounds or voices. You certainly could not get angry about something you aren't listening to anyway.

If it is difficult to think of a piece of music, you could always think of someone whose advice you trust and whose support you value. Give your attention to their voice, making the tone encouraging and supportive. You could give them some words that they might, if they were there, say to you, like,

"What he thinks isn't worth getting wound up about",

"Think of something else until she's gone",

"What are we going to do at the weekend.....",

"She'll go in a minute",

"Don't go getting in trouble because of him he's not worth it"

or, *"Just think of all the things you do well....."*

Chapter 8

As you give your auditory attention to the song or the advisor you cannot also be paying attention to the trigger and this will stop your old response from happening in the way it always did.

One word of caution. If you are trying not to respond angrily to the things a teacher is saying, it may be better to give them your visual attention so that they think you are paying attention.

Visual Triggers - something you see:

A visual trigger is something you see - it might be something like the expression on someone's face, the way they look at you, their swaggering walk or work being crossed out with red pen.

For example, one student I know had "lost it" when a certain teacher looked up from her work and over towards him. Just that visual attention from that particular teacher was enough because in the past, it had been followed by critical comments about his work rate. This student up-ended his desk and stormed out of the classroom as soon as she looked over towards him, even before she had spoken to him about his work - comments that the student expected once again to be critical and disparaging.

Another girl responded time and again to the look on a boy's face, which she interpreted as sneering and deliberately winding her up. Even though she knew he was doing this deliberately, to get her extreme angry reaction, she had been unable to stop her response to the look and "lost it" every time.

If you have been responding to a visual trigger, you need to cut down your old response by giving your visual attention to something else. Look deliberately and with great interest in another direction, preferably so you need to turn your back to the trigger, or simply study your book with great concentration [even if it isn't interesting - pretend it is!].

Another way of distracting your visual attention from a trigger is to imagine that the person is covered by an invisibility cloak. Both the Harry Potter and Lord of the Rings films have included this trick - so if you have seen them, it will be even easier to imagine how this might work for you. It's as if the person isn't there at all. Wrap them in it and blank them out. They are completely invisible. You can't respond to a visual trigger being delivered by someone if you don't notice them even being there.

You must know when to start your chosen visual distraction strategy. The longer you leave it, the harder it is to carry out. You need to watch your film again of a recent incident and notice what happens just before the visual trigger - like when the teacher in the first example put down her pen and sighed just before she started to look up. And like when the boy started to turn his shoulders round from the way he was sitting just before his head also started to turn around in order to sneer. That is just before the visual trigger is delivered to you. The trigger still happens, but by giving your visual attention to something else, you distract yourself from even noticing the trigger happening and so avoid the old inevitable response.

Kinaesthetic Triggers - movements or actions

A kinaesthetic trigger is a movement or action such as deliberately nudging your work, ripping your page, knocking your chair as they walk past you, trying to trip you up or swinging a bag round close to your face. One student I worked with was responding violently to a kinaesthetic trigger. He got wound up when lining up outside a classroom just before going in to start a new lesson. Whenever a certain boy was in the same lessons as him that boy deliberately walked slowly in front of him, not allowing him to get to a place where he wanted to sit and to a friend he wanted to sit near.

The student found this very frustrating and he frequently ended up pushing the other boy away against a wall. The other boy found it all very entertaining but the situation deteriorated when the pushing turned to slapping and punching. The student was in trouble for aggressive and violent behaviour towards the other boy. Of course the other boy suffered no consequences at all - he had just walked slowly after all.

In most cases, it is possible to stop a kinaesthetic trigger from happening, by anticipating it and moving away. Once it has happened, it is too late and you are left with no option but to try to manage your angry response. You need to work out what you need to do so that that doesn't happen. Plan ahead. You need to work out when the trigger happens and what happens just before. Then take avoiding action. Ask if you can change seats, join another group, go to your room, go somewhere different at break times, set off to the classroom just before the bell rings, stand somewhere else, go to a different club or team, go earlier or go later.

All of these strategies are easy and effective. They are carefully and precisely targeted for maximum impact. If you get this bit right, you may never have to do anything else to overcome that old problem you had with anger!

Strategy 3 The Famous Eye-ball Trick!

Useful for:

Any time when you would like to relax instantly. This strategy is especially useful, however, when you are in danger of really "losing it". It stops the process of winding yourself up with unhelpful self-talk very effectively. It also cuts through any **Fight or Flight** response allowing you to stay cool even once you have started getting wound up.
If in the past you have seemed to "lose it" quickly, soon going out of control then this one is for you!

Sit comfortably.

- Now, staring at a point ahead of you, let yourself go day-dreamy, or out of focus. Just like you have been listening to a lesson or TV programme that has been going on for ages, has got boring and your attention is drifting off.

- Keeping your face forwards, allow your eyes to look up so they are comfortably in the top of their sockets. In just a few seconds, now, your eyes may flicker or feel heavy, as if they want to close. And when this happens, just let them close, breathing out at the same time. That's right.

- Keeping your eyes closed, listen to the sound of your own breathing now, slowly and deeply breathing in through your nose and out through your mouth. You may find yourself feeling really switched off and comfortably relaxed already. Open your eyes and go back to the beginning and do that again.

When you feel ready, just keep your eyes closed and allow that relaxed state to continue for about 2 or 3 minutes. You will open up your eyes and feel surprisingly calm and relaxed.

Strategy 4 Square Breathing

Useful for:

Square breathing will help you to relax quickly, at any time. You could use it to calm yourself down at the Feeling Wobbly stage so that your response stays in control. This can stop you from going on through to the Fight or Flight stage. It can also be useful after you have "lost it" to calm down quickly.

To begin, make yourself as comfortable as possible.

Sometimes to help you relax fully while you are doing square breathing, it helps to imagine a place either real or made up - say a beach, garden or by a waterfall. You could think of a place now, before you start and then when you are ready, go there again in your imagination.

Imagine a large square in front of you. In your imagination, count slowly to 4 as you travel along each side in turn.

Now this time add the breathing technique

Side 1 - breathe in as you count slowly to 4
Side 2 - hold your breath for a slow count of 4
Side 3 - let your breath out very slowly as you count to 4
Side 4 - push the rest of the air in your lungs out. You should hear the breath as you squash it all out of your lungs.

Go back to the beginning and do it again. I usually recommend that you do it 4 times through slowly. After even the first time through, you will notice that you feel calmer, still in both mind and body. After 4 times through, you will be perfectly calm and in control of yourself.

Strategy 5 Calm Anchor

Useful for:

This powerful strategy will help you to feel calm instantly. You can use it any time at all but it is most effective if you use it in preparation for difficult situations that used to wind you up, or when you used to feel angry or upset. It will also work instantly for you even when you are really "losing it", to calm down again. It can also be useful after you have "lost it" to calm down again more quickly than usual.

One student I worked with used this strategy most effectively alongside using an Exit Card. His teachers had agreed with me that instead of him constantly losing it in class - it would happen several times a day - they would allow him to leave the classroom when he was starting to get wound up by showing them a coloured card that worked as a pass to get him out of the classroom. They agreed that they would allow him to leave if he needed to and that he would return to class as soon as he had calmed down. We agreed this would take 10-20 minutes but no more. Whilst he was out of the classroom, he agreed to use his Calm Anchor to get himself in the right frame of mind to go calmly back into the classroom and continue with his work.

If you feel this strategy would be useful for you, you could do the reading (pages 51 – 52) in your head or aloud to yourself, or ask someone else to read it aloud to you. However, it may be easier to do if you record it and play it back to yourself so that you can close your eyes and just listen. Speak in a low-toned, patient voice so that it is easy to listen to. You could listen to the recording several times over until you have got the visualisations just right yourself.

Now, everyone can remember at least one time when they were completely calm, can't they? Maybe there are a few different times - you need to think of the best and most vivid memory you have of feeling calm. Just take a few minutes to find the right time, taking yourself back through some memories until you find the right one.

- Go back to that time now when you were completely calm. Remember that time now like watching a film of yourself. It might help to close your eyes and watch that film on the inside of your eyelids or as if on a big screen just in front of you....now notice where you are, any colours you can see, any voices or sounds you can hear nearby or in the distance. Notice your posture, how you move and exactly how you look when you are completely calm.

- Bring the film closer and step into the picture. Step into your own body, look through your own eyes and experience that fully now as if you are really there. Notice the things you can see and hear and especially how completely calm and relaxed you feel now.

- You may find that your breathing has slowed down and become deeper, shoulders relax and facial muscles lose any tension they may have had. That's right. Create a calm anchor now by pressing together your finger and thumb of one hand as that feeling of calmness intensifies even more.

- When you are ready, release the finger and thumb, step out of the picture and open up your eyes bringing all your attention back into the room. As you become fully aware of the room around you now, you may notice that already you are pleasantly calm.

- Repeat that again, next time feeling that calm even more intensely.

So, any time you would like to feel calm all you need to do is connect together the same finger and thumb anchor to access those intensely calm feelings. It is that simple. Try it now, connect the anchor and once again experience that calm state fully and completely.

Now you have your anchor ready to use any time. For this to be effective, you must decide when you will use it, and exactly where and how you will do that.

Strategy 6 Acting 'as if'

Useful for:

Giving others the impression that you are more confident than you are. This will mean that they will not see you as such an easy target, nor will they be so attracted to bullying or mocking you.

Having confidence helps you to bounce back if you are criticised, and defends you from feeling crushed by mockery or bullying. Sometimes just acting "as if" you are confident is enough to help.

I remember teaching this strategy to a boy that was being bullied at school. He was called names, excluded from groups, his school bag was tipped out onto the floor and he was frequently pushed around. He had decided the best way to cope was to try to disappear from everyone's attention, so he would creep around the corridors, duck his head right down and walk as if already flinching from an attack. This didn't work. It made it worse than ever. He needed to be quite brave to try it, but when he "acted as if" he was confident, things improved dramatically very quickly.

We all know when someone is confident - but how do we know? What are the tell tale signs? Think of someone you know that is confident. How do you know? What gives you the impression that they are confident? It might be how they stand or walk, how they speak, how they smile or give eye contact.

Think about that now so that you can give the impression you are confident by taking on some of their mannerisms or behaviours and acting as if you are........Practice makes perfect with this one, so choose something easy to do and start right away. You could add other ideas later until you can easily create exactly the impression you want to create!

Strategy 7 Ring of Confidence

Useful for:

Building your confidence so that you have a clear idea of your positive attributes. When you are confident, you do not get as hurt by the things people say and do. You can be more "resilient" – that is, staying positive even when things don't go exactly to plan, or people say or do things that they intend will hurt you. Being confident creates a barrier between their intention to hurt you and you actually feeling hurt so that you are protected.

Everybody has felt confident at some time during their life have they not?

Think about a time now, any time when you were confident, the most confident you have ever been. Spend a minute or two choosing the right time now and re-live it, noticing what you see, what you hear and how you feel when you are confident. As that feeling builds, imagine a coloured ring on the floor around your feet. Notice its colour now. Notice what colour confidence is. Let the feeling of confidence build, and as it does, let the circle grow and the colours spread, to form a bubble all around you, filling you with that tremendous feeling of confidence now.

Even though you may not have noticed before, confidence may have some music or other sound that indicates how powerful it is. Notice that sound now. Breathe that confidence in deeply now allowing it to spread throughout your whole being - and then double it.

When you are ready, allow the bubble to shrink back down to a coloured ring around your feet again.

Think about a situation when you would like to feel more confident, that will be different when you are confident.

Now just allow the ring to grow again into the coloured bubble. Notice the sounds, colours and feelings surrounding you and filling you with that same tremendous confidence. Imagine that same situation unfold around you with that confidence fully available to you and notice it has changed hasn't it?

Allowing the bubble to shrink back down again, notice how differently you feel about that situation now. That's right!

Any time you could do with feeling more confident, just surround yourself with that coloured bubble.

Strategy 8 Walk Away

Useful for:

Avoiding confrontation and breaking up an old behaviour pattern which could escalate and result in you getting angry and "losing it".

Young people who describe themselves as having an anger management problem often tell me that - "Next time I'll just walk away". However, 9 times out of 10 they don't. They think it would be a good idea to walk away, agree to do it and discuss plans to do it but when they are in a situation where they should carry out their well-meant intentions, they don't do it.

It is a good idea, I agree, because you can't possibly argue or have a confrontation with someone who isn't there. But it very often fails as a strategy.

So, what is the difference that makes the difference? What do you need to do to make this strategy work?

Be very very specific. When you say you are going to walk away what exactly do you mean? Answer these questions:
- Exactly when will you walk away? How will you know when to start walking away? What signals will you notice to let you know when to start? When will you stop?
- Exactly how will you walk away? What will your body language convey as you walk? How fast will you go? Will you stride out or saunter?
- Where will you walk to? Will it be the same place or the same distance away? Is that the best place? Is there an alternative?
- Who will help you or who will you walk to?

- What will you be saying to yourself in your head as you walk? Think of some specific words – what voice will you use?
- Where will you look as you walk?
- What expression will you have on your face?

Practise doing this like watching a film of yourself and keep refining your plan until it is just right. Then try it out for yourself.

Strategy 9 Time Travel

Useful for:

If you have worries, anxieties, things that are playing on your mind, from the past still affecting you now causing you to respond more angrily to triggers than necessary.

If there is something from the past that is worrying you it can cause you to feel on edge, or have a high level of anxiety underlying all your responses and interactions with people. This can mean that your usual responses are turned up and you over-react to triggers that most people could handle. For example one student I worked with had been put up for adoption by her mum when she was a small girl, another had suffered an assault, another had witnessed a road accident in which her friend had died. If you are still badly affected by something that happened in the past your emotional responses may also be turned up, edgy, upset and angry.

In this strategy, I will teach you how to send those feelings back into the past where they belong. Sometimes we carry hurt, upset and anxiety with us for far too long, constantly feeling turned-up emotions that we can't escape from. They don't actually belong to you in the present moment, they belong to the you in the past. Whatever happened still happened and we can't change that, but there is a way of turning those feelings back down to more manageable levels.

If the event that has worried you is a death, then you may still choose to put the emotions you have felt behind you, so that you can cope better and get on with life. However, it is important that in doing so, with care and respect for the person you have lost, you keep whatever it is you need to keep and put behind you only the turned up emotions that are hurting you and are no longer appropriate. This helped me, when I lost my dad.

Now sit comfortably. We are going to travel back in time to visit your past. Imagine that the past stretches out behind you like a time-line or pathway. Turn your chair to look along the line. Far away along the line is you when you were a baby. Closer to you, there are recent events that have just happened. Some distance away from you now, notice that event back in the past that has been affecting you. We cannot change what happened, but we can change how you feel about it now. Send those turned up emotions back along the line to where they belong, as if along a zip-wire or slide.

Now in your imagination, as if travelling in a hot air balloon go high up and back along the line to that moment just before the event happened. It is important that you are high up - as high as you can go. Check that you have travelled back to before the event now and land your balloon there. Notice that you are at a time before you had experienced those turned up emotions and notice where those emotions are now - that's right, in the event. Just check they are there instead of with you. Leave them there.

When you are ready, once again in your imagination travel high up in your hot air balloon, back to the present and bring all your attention back into the room. And those emotions have gone haven't they? Good.

Strategy 10 Stand in their Shoes

Useful for:

If there is somebody that you argue with or disagree with in some way that makes you feel angry, this strategy will help you to understand what they are thinking and feeling. It may also help you to think about them in a different way so that you can do something a bit differently.

Think about an occasion when you and this person were arguing or disagreeing about something. Watch it like a film through your own eyes. Notice how you look, the things you say and how you say them, your posture and body language. Do the same for the other person. Look through your own eyes at them and notice the same things.

Now move around to another spot in the room and this time step in to the other person's shoes and watch the same film but through their eyes. Become them for a moment and notice how you look, the things you do, what you say, and how you say it. Notice how they look through their own eyes, how they move and how they sound.

Now step away again and having looked thoughtfully at the situation from both perspectives, move around to another spot in the room and look at the incident as if you were a fly on the wall, not knowing either person. What do you notice about both of them and the disagreement they are having?

Finally step back into your own shoes and take with you the insights you have gained just now. Think about these questions. You don't have to answer them fully, just think about them. What have you learned about you? How was the situation different through the other person's eyes? What have you learned about them? What could you do differently to change what used to happen?

Information, Telephone Numbers and Websites

Young Minds

The website www.youngminds.org.uk has lots of information on mental health issues affecting young people. The information booklet "Feeling angry?" is part of a range of booklets written for the 11-16 year age range. Written for young people whose anger is making things difficult for them, this booklet explains that we all feel angry sometimes but that it's how we express anger that can lead to problems. The booklet explores, amongst other things, what makes us feel this way and also suggests how to recognise these angry feelings. It looks at what we can do when we feel angry and how to get help if these feelings are overwhelming.

Childline

www.childline.org.uk
The UK's 24 hour helpline for children and young people with any problem. Lines can be busy, but you should keep trying. **0800 1111** or write to Childline at **Freepost 1111**

Careline

A confidential crisis telephone counselling for children, young people and adults. Careline can refer callers to other organisations and support groups throughout the country. **020 8514 1177**
[Mon to Fri 10am to 4pm and 7pm to 10pm]

Bullying

www.kidscape.org.uk
Kidscape offers great advice on bullying and how to avoid it.

Sexwise

A free and confidential helpline on sex, relationships and contraception for young people in the UK. **0800 282930** [7am to 12 midnight daily]

Domestic Violence	The Hideout website www.thehideout.org.uk is the first national website to support children and young people living with domestic violence, or those who may want to help a friend. The site informs children and young people about domestic violence and can help you identify whether it is happening in your home.
Drugs	**www.ndh.org.uk** The National Drugs Helpline offers information and advice to anyone in the UK concerned about drugs. The 24-hour service is free and confidential. **0800 776600** [24-hour, daily]
Family Splitting Up	Are you worried that your parents are splitting up? If so, the children's charity NCH has a website www.itsnotyourfault.org which might help you understand what's happening and feel a bit better.
Bullying Online	Provides email advice about bullying, and tries to respond to all emails within 24 hours. To email Bullying Online visit **www.bullying.co.uk**
Alcohol Concern	Has lots of information and advice on drinking and alcohol related problems on its website at: **www.alcoholconcern.org.uk**
Child and Adolescent Mental Health Services	This free NHS service may be contacted on a regional basis through the family's own GP. The Young Minds website explains the system very well and offers a national directory of services on **www.youngminds.org.uk/camhs**

My interest in Anger Management first developed when my own daughter suffered a violent attack at school. I became aware that there is a shocking number of such incidents in schools and that there are too few resources in place to overcome and prevent them. This book is intended to help fill that gap.

For further information in these areas:-

- Crisis Intervention
  1-1 support for a young person

- Consultations for parents, carers, or mentoring professionals

- INSET and professional development courses

Contact Carol on 01995 605019 or email **carol@achieve4u.org**